COMPACT DISC PAGE AND BAND INFORMATION

MMO CD 3324
MMO Cass. 8004

LAUREATE SERIES CONTEST SOLOS
INTERMEDIATE LEVEL FOR FLUTE, VOL. 2

Band No. Complete Version			Band No. Minus Flute	Page No.
1	BACH: Suite in B minor -	Polonaise	10	6
2		Badinerie	11	7
		Badinerie (Slow Version)	12	7
3	BAKSA: Aria Da Capo		13	8
4	MARCELLO:			
	Sonata in F major -	Adagio	14	10
5		Allegro	15	10
		Allegro (Slow Version)	16	10
6		Largo	17	12
7		Allegro	18	12
		Allegro (Slow Version)	19	12
8	WIDOR: Scherzo -	Allegro vivace	20	14
		Allegro vivace (Slow Version)	21	14
9	Piano Tuning Notes			

LS LAUREATE SERIES

FLUTE MUSIC BOOK

TUNING
Before the piano accompaniment begins you will hear four tuning notes, followed by a short scale and another tuning note. This will enable you to tune your instrument to the record.

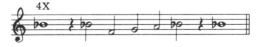

PERFORMANCE GUIDE
COMMENTARY BY DONALD PECK
BACH
Suite in B Minor: Polonaise and Badinerie

The Bach Suites are based on dance forms; they must not sound academic. This Polonaise should be bright and lilting. Work for contrast in the repeats; the first repeat can be played softly. The accompaniment carries the melodic interest in the Trio. Listen carefully; the flute part is merely a florid obligato. If you accent the runs slightly they will not sound like a blur.

The Badinerie should be very jolly. If you think the rhythm in a fast four, it will have a jaunty, jogging feeling. The dynamics should appear *subito.* If you feel certain notes need a special stress, you might try slurring them. This technique will help you to arrive at a practical articulation.

BAKSA   Aria da Capo

Study this music carefully; the composer, Robert Baksa has indicated exactly what he wants. Your attention to rhythm should be especially meticulous. Compare measures 31 and 33:

Notice how much lighter the triplet pick-up in bar 33 feels. The pick-up to measure 60, and eighth note and four sixteenths, gives a sense of urgency as you *decrescendo* into measure 60.

The passage beginning in measure 55 is an ornamentation of the main theme. Follow the dynamic suggestions and play cleanly. The result should be a lovely, flowing Aria.

MARCELLO
Sonata in F Major

The Adagio is difficult to play smoothly because of the thirty second notes. If you play it too fast, it will sound very rough. You must have an even flow. You might practice by sustaining the F natural as if it were a whole note throughout the bar. Just think the written notes and intensify your support. Then, when you play the passage as written, move your fingers for the pitch changes, but don't try to phrase. This technique should help you to make an even transition. The important thing is to keep your air flowing. In performance, of course, you will want to play a little more *dolce.* If your preparation has been thorough, you should be able to color your tone without disturbing the line. Whenever you have a repeated section, you should give the piece variety by altering the dynamics, playing with a more open tone, or adding embellishments. The trill in measure 3 might be played:

The second movement is light and graceful. You will not need a sharp attack. Play with a very light "duh" tongue, and the sixteenth notes will be crisp enough. Allow the theme to have a good lilt. The dynamic levels

in baroque music are usually rather abrupt. This may be because most of this music was written for the harpsichord, which cannot crescendo. Try building your dynamics in a series of "terraces." Play the descending sixteenth notes in measure *8 piano.* The next sequence could be *mezzoforte,* and the last one in measure 9 *forte.* If you play it this way, without a crescendo, you will add a truly authentic touch!

The Largo demands an exquisite, ethereal sound without losing its austerity. The phrase beginning with the second beat of measure 8 is echoed by the phrase beginning with the last beat of measure 10. Do not play the trills too fast; an evenly measured shake would be ideal. The trill in measure 9 might have been written:

The Allegro in 12/8 is light and happy. You must play it accurately, but without stress on every important beat. There is a fine opportunity to "terrace" your dynamic levels. Play the repeated A's in measure 14 *forte,* the G's in measure 16 *mezzoforte,* and the E's in measure 18 *piano.* Practice will make the transition from one dynamic to the next smooth and effective.

WIDOR
Scherzo, Op. 34, No. 2

Breathing is very difficult in this piece. Whenever you have a chance, take a breath, even if you think you don't need it. It may help to hold the first note of a phrase slightly and then rush the notes which follow. This will give you a chance to breathe at the end of the phrase. This technique must never be apparent to your audience! You can use melodic accents in this music, done with the air and the vibrato, not with the tongue. Always remember that Scherzos are playful; this is not necessarily achieved through speed. If you choose a slower tempo, you will have more time to take bigger breaths. Work for an easy, relaxed quality. This is not an easy piece, but most rewarding!

Donald Peck

SUITE IN B MINOR

Polonaise

J. S. BACH

Badinerie

ARIA DA CAPO

ROBERT F. BAKSA
1957

SONATA IN F MAJOR

BENEDETTO MARCELLO

(senza rall.)

SCHERZO

CHARLES M. WIDOR, Op. 34, No. 2

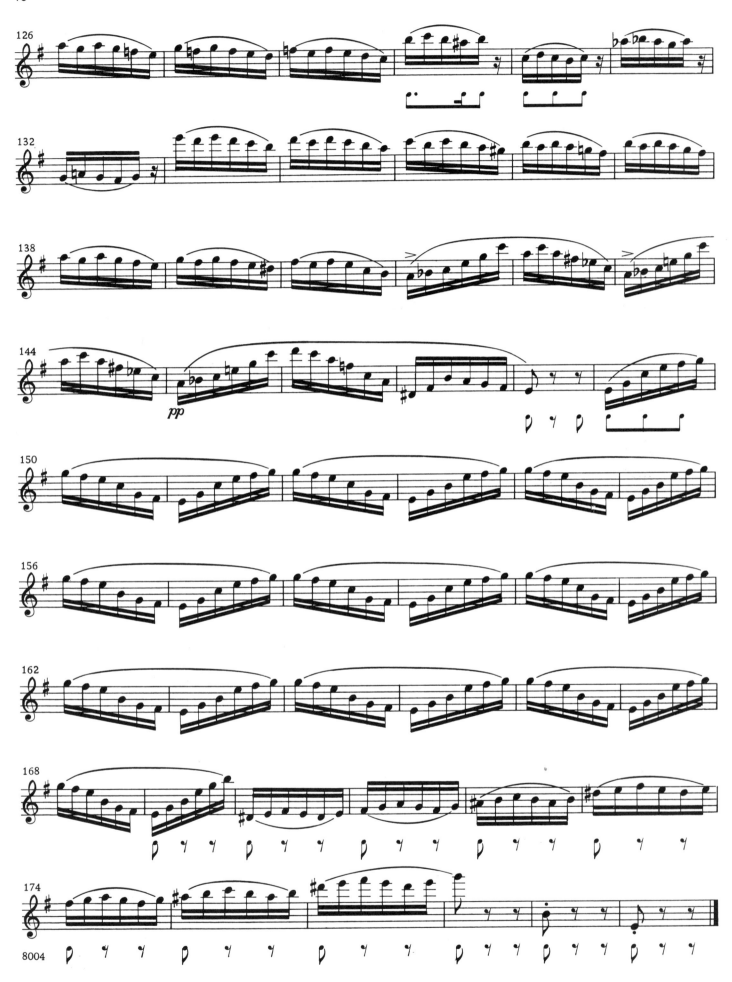

MUSIC MINUS ONE 50 Executive Boulevard • Elmsford New York 10523-1325